Lent 2021

Recomended
priest in charge
a copy given to Pe[...]
broth day 2021. He [...]
came to an exhib[...]   He
for Mission in   [...]omotion
Some poetry. He is priest at The [...]owed   and read

church Cambridge
and chaplin of [...] College.

The Singing Bowl

The Singing Bowl

MALCOLM GUITE

CANTERBURY
PRESS
Norwich

© Malcolm Guite 2013

First published in 2013 by the Canterbury Press Norwich
Editorial office
3rd Floor, Invicta House,
108–114 Golden Lane,
London EC1Y 0TG

Canterbury Press is an imprint of
Hymns Ancient & Modern Ltd (a registered charity)
13A Hellesdon Park Road, Norwich,
Norfolk, NR6 5DR, UK

www.canterburypress.co.uk

Fourth impression 2020

All rights reserved. No part of this publication may be
reproduced, stored in a retrieval system, or transmitted,
in any form or by any means, electronic, mechanical,
photocopying or otherwise, without the prior permission
of the publisher, Canterbury Press.

The Author has asserted his right under the
Copyright, Designs and Patents Act, 1988, to be
identified as the Author of this Work.

British Library Cataloguing in Publication data

A catalogue record for this book is available
from the British Library

978 1 84825 541 8

Typeset by Regent Typesetting, London
Printed and bound in Great Britain by
CPI Group (UK) Ltd, Croydon, CR0 4YY

Contents

Part II The Four Loves

Part III Word and World

Part VI Three Sequences

Preface

In *Sounding the Seasons* I concentrated on a single form, the sonnet, and made a journey through the year in a sequence of poems intended to sound and celebrate the mysteries of faith. In *The Singing Bowl* I range more widely, in subject, style, and poetic form, and faith is as much, if not more, at the roots of the poetry than in its branches and blossom. Indeed the sense of being rooted and earthed is an essential element in this collection. The title poem is not my invocation of the muse but rather her admonition to me:

> Begin the song exactly where you are.
> Remain within the world of which you're made.
> Call nothing common in the earth or air.

This is her counsel about both poetry and prayer and in the poems that follow I am trying both to celebrate the world of which I'm made, finding 'Heaven in ordinary', and also to discern and echo a little of its music.

This collection therefore begins with a section called 'Local Habitations', evocations of particular places with their own peculiar virtues, though some of these earthly places are, in their own ways, gates of Heaven.

We love local habitations also for the people who inhabit them, and the second part of this book, 'The Four Loves', borrows its title from C.S. Lewis's exploration of our four-fold loving, from friendship to familiar affection, from *Eros* to *Agape*.

Part Three, 'Word And World', reflects on the art of poetry itself and more widely on how language involves us with one another, how it both deepens and limits our knowledge. It is also about *techne* understood both as technique in art and also the technology that has transformed the way we communicate. It closes with the 'found' sonnet 'Imagine', drawn entirely from phrases in C.S. Lewis's prophetic book *The Abolition of Man*, a book which foresees some of the darker places our technology might take us and calls us back to a language and science that might make us more truly human.

Both people and poems become more completely themselves when they find their true form, work within their limits, and concentrate their power within what Blake called 'the bounding line'. One bounding line, essential to all things abounding here, is the line of death itself, and Philip Larkin rightly warned us against 'the costly aversion of the eyes from death'. Part Four of this collection, 'Intimations of Mortality' offers some unaverted meditation on love and loss.

It is followed however by a section called 'Clouds of Witness', for beyond death's bounding line there is another music, and even as we remain within the world of which we're made, we can hear, still resonant, the songs of those who went before. In *Sounding the Seasons* I wrote sonnets for some of the saints, but restricted myself to those named in the Bible. In this section I offer a sonnet sequence celebrating some other saints, especially of these islands, and also those not formally sainted but surely of the household of faith. Many of them have their 'days' in the Christian Year and so this sequence can be read as an extension of *Sounding The Seasons* and used in similar ways. But we return from Heaven to Earth at the end of this section with *Descent*, a poem in English Sapphics, on the Incarnation.

Finally, I conclude the book with three short poetic sequences. The first, *Canon C.26:1*, is a sonnet sequence about wrestling with difficulty in prayer and persisting through it. *Six Glimpses* also takes up some of the 'problem of evil' and suffering touched on in *Canon C.26*. As a form, the sestina requires the poet constantly to return to the same set of six words, and in the first five poems I use that form to give a glimpse of five people in crisis, turning and returning upon their particular pain. The final sestina offers a glimpse of someone who turns and returns in the redemptive repetition of prayer, to those same points of crisis, praying for the five people whom she has glimpsed during her day. Again it is about persistence rather than 'answers'.

The opening poem of the final sequence *On Reading the* Commedia returns to a line from the title poem, again as a word from the muse. This sequence of nine poems in terza rima takes the reader on a journey with Dante through the three realms. But it is not so much about Dante's journey as about the new journey we ourselves make with every reading of his poem, about the way in which his Hell, Purgatory, and Paradise turn out always to be such telling and centring maps of our own souls. Whilst these poems are written in conversation with Dante's great text I hope it is also possible to read them in the present tense and taste them on our own tongue, without a detailed knowledge of the *Commedia*.

The poem 'Singing Bowl' asks both reader and writer to listen for and stay with a certain kind of music. In all the variety of subject matter, tone and poetic form within this collection I have tried, as far as possible, to hear and to express a song, a singing line.

Malcolm Guite

Cambridge
June 2013

Acknowledgements

Acknowledgements are due to the editors of the following publications in which some of these poems have appeared:

Live Simply, Canterbury Press (2008), *The Ambler*, *The Mars Hill Review*, *The Temenos Academy Review*, *Parabola*, *The Persimmon Review*, *The Tower*.

A number of these poems also appeared in two privately printed chapbooks:

Saying the Names (2002), *The Magic Apple Tree* (2004).

'Descent' was first published as a song on the CD 'Keening for the Dawn' by Steve Bell.

This collection is drawn from poems written over a number of years and I am grateful for the support and encouragement of friends and family in the course of writing them. The Girton College Poetry Group has been an especially helpful forum in which to try out and develop first versions of some of these poems.

Singing Bowl

Begin the song exactly where you are.
Remain within the world of which you're made.
Call nothing common in the earth or air.

Accept it all and let it be for good.
Start with the very breath you breathe in now,
This moment's pulse, this rhythm in your blood

And listen to it, ringing soft and low.
Stay with the music, words will come in time.
Slow down your breathing. Keep it deep and slow.

Become an open singing bowl, whose chime
Is richness rising out of emptiness,
And timelessness resounding into time.

And when the heart is full of quietness
Begin the song exactly where you are.

Part I

Local Habitations

In Bewley's

I look up, hands around my coffee cup,
On Grafton Street in Bewley's coffee shop;
Blue Mountain, *Java* and *Colombian*,
The labels are a journey on their own.
Then the aroma as they're ground by hand,
Broken and opened, out of every land,
Separate savours float across this room
Of dark mahogany, to a softer bloom
Of stained glass windows, where I sit apart
Warming my hands, and waiting on my heart
To call me to adventure. I have found my voice,
Yeats in my pocket, backpack full of Joyce.
I'm nineteen. It is nineteen seventy-seven,
And Dublin is the very gate of heaven.

On The Great Blasket

In a ring of rocks on a cliff's edge by the sea,
Caught by the cold, the amorous wind of the north,
And by a desire that is dying and seeking re-birth
In a ring of rocks on a cliff's edge by the sea.

Detail of fern and heather, vacant sky,
This windblown abstract gallery of stones,
A place inspected by the sea-gull's eye,
A place of beasts and saints, and whitening bones.

A place apart, marked out, a ring of Faith,
Each rock piled round by thin, ascetic hands,
Where I glimpse the fleeting hare,
Where sea-birds call,
Here, saint and devil fought,
And angels there.
Held in my silver-ringed, sun-reddened hands
The gesture, not the substance of a prayer.

Keats's House, Rome

The sun strikes gold along the Spanish Steps,
Patches of god-light where the tourists stray.
The old house is in shadow and still keeps
Its treasures from the searching light of day.
I found it once, when I had lost my way,
Depressed and restless, sheltering from rain,
Long years ago in Rome. But from that day
Everything turned to gold, even my pain,
Reading the words of one who feared he wrote in
    vain.

I too was 'half in love with ease-full death',
And standing by the window, near his bed,
I almost heard the tender-taken breath
On which his words were forming. As I read
I felt things shifting in me, an old dread
Was somehow being brought to harmony,
Taught by his music as the music fled,
To sing at last, as by some alchemy
Despair was lifted slowly into poetry.

I spent that summer there and came each day
To read and breathe and let his life unfold
In mine, till gradually I made my way
From realms of darkness into realms of gold,
Finding that in his story mine was told;
Bereavements, doubts and longings, all were there

Somehow transmuted in the poem's old
Enduring crucible, that furnace where
Quick-silver draws the gold from leaden-eyed
  despair.

Now with the sun I come on pilgrimage
To find this house and climb the foot-worn stair,
For I have lived to more than twice his age
And year-by-year his words have helped me bear
The black weight of my breathing, to repair
An always-breaking heart. Somehow he keeps
His watch on me from somewhere, that bright
  star ...
So, with the words of one who mined the depths,
I sing and strike for gold along the Spanish Steps.

Saying the Names, Warkworth Harbour

Dawn over Amble, and along the coast
Light on the tide flows to Northumberland,
Silvers the scales of herring freshly caught
And gleaming in their boxes on the dock,
Shivers the rainbow sheen on drops of diesel,
And lights at last the North Sea fishing fleet.
Tucked into harbour here, their buoyant lines
Lift to the light on plated prows their names,
The ancient names picked out in this year's paint:
Providence, *Bold Venture*, *Star Divine*
Are first along the quay-side. *Fruitful Bough*
Has stemmed the tides to bring her harvest in,
Orcadian Mist and *Sacred Heart*, *Aspire*,
Their names are numinous, a found poem.
Those Bible-burnished phrases live and lift
Into the brightening tide of morning light
And beg to be recited, chanted out,
For names are incantations, mysteries
Made manifest like ships on the horizon.
Eastward their long line tapers towards dawn
And ends at last with *Freedom*, *Radiant Morn*.

Cowper's View, All Saints Hartford

So this was 'Cowper's View', this open stretch
Of the Great Ouse. Did he stand here and gaze
As I do from the church porch to the river
With its flood-meadows holding scraps of sky?
Did he reflect upon the sun's reflection
In running water held so strong and still,
Both in and on the stream and yet beyond,
Beyond its changing surface and its depth?
And if he stood, like me, upon this path
To watch the sun that watches from the stream
And wonder, was he waiting then, as now
I wait and watch? What was he waiting for?
A lifting of the darkness or the veil?
God knows the light was dark enough for him.
Did he stand here in deepening despair,
Numb to the world around, or did he find
A something in the sun reflected here
And in the stream and in the widening sky
That just might edge an opening when the lid,
The tight black lid of darkness closed on him?
Or was it just the same for him as me
When darkness comes and nothing seems to matter?

Whatever he was waiting for it came
With death, and after death, or not at all.
And so I wait with him and all the rest,
The rest who wait and rest on holy ground

(The dedication here is to All Saints).
They wait and rest but I am restless waiting.
I wait today for this day's funeral,
For I am vicar here and I stand in,
Stand in and speak for those who cannot speak,
Stand in and pray for those who cannot pray,
Stand in and weep for those who cannot weep.
I wait this day for this day's funeral,
As vicars waited here in Cowper's day,
And I am witness to the river's flow,
A witness to the passing of each drop
Of light and life, however sweet or slow.
I see it go; I watch it borne away,
Borne on the backs of bearers as they come
Slow-footing up the path to where I stand.
I stand here for the Stand-In, he who comes
To bear with us as we are borne away.
Though born before us, on the cross he bears
The black weight for us all and bares our hearts.
Cowper's he bears, and mine, and now with me
Bears the poor body under this black lid.
He goes and flows with us and yet he stays;
His life is light upon our shadowed stream.
He is the sun and it is his reflection
That shines in us and also shines beyond,
Beyond these lives that once refracted light
And also have endured the coming dark.

And so the funeral starts. Again we praise
Each passing life and grieve that it should pass
So swiftly to an end. The day is over,
But still I wait and watch the setting sun
Whose dying light is blessing 'Cowper's View'.

I wait and watch its watery reflection,
I watch with Cowper through my darkened days,
And wait with him till we shall see sunrise.

Southwell Leaves

Amidst the tympanum
His stone hair startles from
A face in the foliage.
Not just the bearded barleycorn
But a whole field springing,
The vine and all its tendrils,
Unfold from the face,
Trip from the tongue
That speaks the Word
Amidst the tympanum.

But by the rood-screen here,
His face is set like flint,
The Word unheard,
He gives his back to the smiters
His cheeks to them that pluck out the hair,
His spring is come to shame and spitting,
Under the blows the cut stones splinter
The Green Man comes to winter,
To the harness and the harrow
As flails fall to split the bearded husk
And seeds fall to the furrow,
Amidst the tympanum,
Hard by the rood-screen here.

York Minster

I walked upon your walls in late November
As bonfires flickered in the minster garden,
The smoke of smouldering leaves beset your stones
And withered in a drifting swirl of mist
Through which I glimpsed the ghosts of other
    flames,
The burnings of another age's winter.
I saw your blackened beams against the snow,
And dragon longships, frozen in the Ouse,
The Blood-Axe and his kindred bearing torches,
Wading ashore from off the wasted whale-road.

In you they found a vulnerable haven.
The subtle windings of their swimming tongue
Uncoiled at last in your accepting peace.
Your loosened blood has patiently out-loved them,
Has blessed and broken every pagan heart.
Their scattered bones are flaxen English seed,
Frika and Freya, Loki of the flames,
Woden hanging nine days on the tree
Wooed by the Word, at last succumbed to you.

York Minster, broken bone-house, broken home
Of broken bread, in all your funeral rites
You witness Resurrection. Seven times
Your skeleton has crumbled into ash.
Alive impossibility, remember,

Remember us, your unremembering children.
Stand up old stones, hold in your bones the light,
The dispensation to each piling year
Of Love's abiding truth. Treasure your relics,
And in the pitch of penitential psalms
Prepare a place to keep your people safe
Before the flaming of the final siege.

Hatley St George

Stand here awhile and drink the silence in.
Where clear glass lets in living light to touch
And bless your eyes, a beech tree's tender green
Shimmers beyond the window's lucid arch.
You look across an absent sanctuary;
No walls or roof, just holy, open space,
Leading your gaze out to the fresh-leaved beech
God planted here before you first drew breath.

Stand here awhile and drink the silence in.
You cannot stand as long and still as these,
This ancient beech and still more ancient church.
So let them stand, as they have stood, for you.
Let them disclose their gifts of time and place,
A secret kept for you through all these years.
Open your eyes. This empty church is full,
Thronging with life and light your eyes have missed.

Stand here awhile and drink the silence in.
Shields of forgotten chivalry, and rolls
Of honour for the young men gunned at Ypres,
And other monuments of our brief lives
Stand for the presence here of saints and souls
Who stood where you stand, to be blessed like you;
Clouds of witness to unclouded light
Shining this moment, in this place for you.

Stand here awhile and drink their silence in.
Annealed in glass, the twelve Apostles stand
And each of them is keeping faith for you.
This roof is held aloft, to give you space,
By graceful angels praying night and day
That you might hear some rumour of their flight,
That you might feel the flicker of a wing
And let your heart fly free at last in prayer.

Communion Table, St Edward's, Cambridge

The centuries have settled on this table,
Deepened the grain beneath a clean white cloth
Which bears afresh our changing elements.
Year after year of prayer, in hope and trouble,
Were poured out here and blessed and broken, both
In aching absence and in absent presence.

This table too the earth herself has given
And human hands have made. Where candle-flame
At corners burns and turns the air to light
The oak once held its branches up to heaven,
Blessing the elements which it became,
Rooting the dew and rain, branching the light.

Because another tree can bear, unbearable
For us, the weight of Love, so can this table.

Out in the Elements, Grantchester

I crunch the gravel on my ravelled walks
And clabber with my boots in the wet clay
For I myself am clay that breathes and talks
Articulated earth, I move and pray,
Alive at once to walk and be the way.
The root beneath, the branch above the tree
These hedges bright with blossom, white with May,
Everything concentrates, awaits in me
The coming of the One who sets creation free.

Earth opens now to sudden drumming rains,
The raised and falling waters of the sea
Whose tidal pull and play is in my veins
Spilling and spreading, filling, flowing free,
Whose ebb and flow is still at work in me
And in the wombing pulse of play and work
When heartbeats pushed in waves of empathy
Till waters broke and bore me from the dark
And found this foundered shore and took me from
    the ark.

As rain recedes I pause to fill my pipe
And kindle fire that flickers into light
And lights the leaf all curled and cured and ripe
Within a burr-starred bowl. How fierce and bright
It glows against the cold. And I delight
In taste and fragrance, watching wisps of grey

And graceful smoke in their brief flight,
As sun breaks from the clouds and lights my way
I feel the fire that makes the light that makes the
   day.

Now air is all astir in breaks and blasts,
The last grey rags of cloud are blown aside
The hedgerows hush and rustle in the gusts
As clean winds whistle round me. Far and wide
Bent grasses and frail flowers lean aside.
I breathe the world in with this brimming breeze
That tugs at me and eddies at my side,
Quickens and flickers through the tangled trees
And breathes me back to life and brings me to my
   knees.

Akin to every creature I will learn
From each and all the meaning of my birth.
I love the dust to which I will return,
The subtle substance of my mother earth,
From water born, by fire fathered forth,
An index and epitome of nature,
I sum and summon all the world is worth,
And breathing now His elemental air
I find the One within, without, and everywhere.

The Magic Apple Tree, The Fitzwilliam Museum, Cambridge

Someday make a journey through the rain,
Through sodden streets in darkening December:
A journey to the magic apple tree.
And journey also, darkling, through your past.
Journey through your seed time and your summer
And through the fall of every fruiting time.
Journey through the pictures packed like loam,
The rooting places of your growing soul,
The subsoil of your oldest memory.
Walk through the outer darkness of the world
Towards a buried memory of light
Whose faded trace no photograph records.
You glimpsed it once within the garden wall,
The image of an ancient apple tree,
The fall of light through branches and the fling
And curve of colour on the golden fruit ...
All buried in the rubble of your fall.

Walk through the present darkness till you come
To the stone steps, the lions, the façade,
The white Museum with its plate-glass doors.
Through these you pass and up a flight of stairs,
To find the case and lift the dull brown cover
To see, at first, your image in the glass.
You see yourself, and through yourself the tree,
And through the tree at last, the buried light.

Boughs form an arch, the painting draws you in
Under its framing fringe of rich green leaves,
Beyond the music of the shepherdess,
Down through the dark towards the grey church
    spire
Into its heart : the arching apple boughs ...
The sky is dark, intense, a stormy grey,
But just beneath the darkness all is gold:
The slope of hills, the fields of barleycorn.
The loaded branches of the apple tree,
Glow red and ripe and gold and bow themselves
To bless the fruitful earth from whence they spring.
These colours seem to fall from Eden's light,
The air they shine through breathes a change in
    them,
Breaking their sheen into a certain shade
Particular and unrepeatable.
Some golden essence seems to concentrate
From light to air, from pigment into paint
In increments of incarnation down
To burn within these apples and this bough,
Which here and now at last, you recognise.
This is your own, your ancient apple tree
And here the light you buried for so long
Leaps up in you to life and resurrection.

First Steps, Brancaster

This is the day to leave the dark behind you,
Take the adventure, step beyond the hearth,
Shake off at last the shackles that confined you,
And find the courage for the forward path.
You yearned for freedom through the long night
    watches,
The day has come and you are free to choose,
Now is your time and season.
Companioned still by your familiar crutches
And leaning on the props you hope to lose,
You step outside and widen your horizon.

After the dimly burning wick of winter
That seemed to dull and darken everything
The April sun shines clear beyond your shelter
And clean as sight itself. The reed-birds sing,
As heaven reaches down to touch the earth
And circle her, revealing everywhere
A lovely, longed-for blue.
Breathe deep and be renewed by every breath,
Kinned to the keen east wind and cleansing air,
As though the blue itself were blowing through you.

You keep the coastal path where edge meets edge,
The sea and salt marsh touching in North Norfolk,
Reed cutters cuttings, patterned in the sedge,
Open and ease the way that you will walk,

Unbroken reeds still wave their feathered fronds
Through which you glimpse the long line of the sea
And hear its healing voice.
Tentative steps begin to break your bonds,
You push on through the pain that sets you free,
Towards the day when broken bones rejoice.

Cloud-Hidden, San Francisco

For Gerry Nicosia

I flew to San Francisco
And took the rainbow bus
Further into otherness
And further into us.

Further into ecstasy
And further into pain,
Further than those acid tests
And all this acid rain.

I climbed the stairs in City Lights
And tried the poet's chair,
My verses formed a golden gate
That shimmered in mid air.

My verses hung a bridge between
Those Dharma days and mine,
Suspended between heav'n and earth,
Tense in every line.

Snyder breathes the mountain air
Where mountains walk alone,
Ferlinghetti's breathing still,
Tho' Ginsberg is long gone:

His chants are still vibrating
Beyond his final bow,
He howls a hipster's Sanctus
With hidden angels now.

And Cassady is everywhere,
Garcia's in my head;
I'm grateful just to be alive
To hear the Grateful Dead.

I read with Nicosia, read
The faces and the streets;
I beat these pavements with the man
Who chronicled the Beats.

We touch St Peter and St Paul
Where Jack and Neal both prayed
And Dante's writing on the wall
Says all that can be said.

Tonight we read in Berkley,
Tomorrow in North Beach
We'll harmonise with mermaids,
Still singing each to each.

The skyline writes an epitaph
With every vapour trail,
As Gerry reads his elegies
For every vet* in jail.

_____

* A reference to Gerry Nicosia's work with imprisoned war veterans.

And after in Vesuvio's
We drink a few for Jack
While Tom says to 'fare forward'
And Van sings 'take me back'.

I try to read the glimmer,
The strange pearlescent light,
That graces San Francisco skies
And presages the night,

And find myself cloud-hidden,
Where rhythms never stop,
Cloud-hidden with the poets
On the foggy mountain top.

Westward

We're looking west to where our setting sun,
Already out of sight, looks back at us, to fling
His dying splendour to these clouds. They burn
With borrowed gold and crimson, not their own
Like strips of silk torn from his royal robe,
These flags of hope left by our solar king,
Who sinks for us below the dark horizon
That he might yet encompass all this globe.

He leaves us with the promise of his rising
For all we face the west of his decline
Already somewhere else are voices praising
As on the east they glimpse a kindled line.
His setting is a herald of the morn,
We watch the sunset, but we tread the dawn.

Part II

The Four Loves

Glances

For Maggie and Cathy

Down from the Green Man, where the meadow
    starts,
And through the meadow to the running stream
We saunter into summer side by side,
The three of us, and watch as three swans glide
Like some heraldic emblem in a dream
That only opens up to open hearts.
Walking between you everything I see
Is doubled and redoubled through your eyes
And through the words and silences we share,
And everything is gift! I stop and stare.
Everything dances, everything! Surprise
Glances between you both, glances to me,
And glances from the child in me who stands
Unseen between us almost holding hands.

Must I disrupt my life with discipline?

Must I disrupt my life with discipline,
Defer the invitations of each empty page
To be haranguing myself in Lowell's tone
Desiring the advantage of his age,
To be like Li Po, drunk with rice-wine, vague,
Reeling before reflections of the moon,
Defer these things for nothing, for the maze
Of a dead language, an incomprehensible grammar,
Whose centre holds a blind bull-headed scholar?
Rather let me stammer through these nights
Making a fertile garden of my squalor
Where we can scatter seeds in spring and raise
Above the rhythm of our appetites
The strange quietus I had thought was love.

Lying Alone

Lying alone in pale electric light
I furl my warmth into the freezing air.
Mirror on mirror mirrors white on white,
Far and then near and near again and far.
And nothing is where their reflections are
And there is nothing here that is not mine
And I shall hear before the lights go out
A final echo fading from the stair
As darkness gathers till my room is full.
Above the pillow then whose breath will stir?
From the deserted bathroom who will call?
Memory traces down a delicate line,
Her fingers barely touching, a soft fall
Of snow upon the ridges of my spine.

Wedding Day

For Joanna and Nicholas

'If anyone is in Christ there is a new creation.'
2 Cor. 5:17

Now you have come at last to the first day
Inside that Love whose end is to begin.
Circles and spirals find their hidden way
Home to this centre where they hold and stay.
Old lives renew and quicken from within,
Love is the fountain in whose flow and play
All that you are is cleansed of every stain.
Singly you die and doubly live again.

Joy is alive in you like hidden grain
Open and growing in your common life
As you become each other's dew and rain
Nurturing God's good garden. Man and wife,
Now and forever, stand before your Lord
And be created by his Living Word.

Hand in Hand: Kerouac and Cassady

For Kevin Flanagan

He walks up to a door in Spanish Harlem,
The door is opened by a naked man,
That's it for Jack and Neal, the party starts ...
Playing with veils they never knew were there,
Catholic kids who left the church for joy,
Since Joy seemed to have left the church before them.
They figured they could chase her down between
    them,
Somewhere in the chaos, in the maelstrom,
Somewhere in the words that come at midnight,
The wine, the pills, the angel-headed hipsters,
The all-night drives, the ecstasy of jazz,
Unspoken loyalties, betrayals, broken vows,
She'd be there somewhere, in some other car
On someone else's sofa, in some bar,
Or somewhere on the road right up ahead,
Surely two boys like these could track her down.
But she was always gone before they got there ...

And still I see them walking through the fog,
Too close for comfort where the breakers roll,
And North Beach sirens sing their songs of love.
They're too far gone in love to understand,
Drunk on the closeness of the naked soul,
But joy still whispers 'All, all shall be well,
We're all going to heaven hand in hand.'

Midnight

We had postponed it many times,
Fearing the end such means begin,
Yet midnight's long awaited chimes
Saw shuttered moonlight stripe our skin.

Recalling that ecstatic rage,
The moving bars of light and shade,
My mind becomes a shabby cage
To hold the tiger-love we made.

We have denied it many times,
In separate complacency,
But still at midnight, weighted chimes
Conspire to set our creature free.

Is it a memory or another dream?

Is it a memory or another dream
That golden afternoon in which we walk
Together through the meadow? Touch and talk
Are mingled as we sit beside the stream
And watch the minnows swim against the flow.
They dart between dark shadows and the gleam
Of sunlight in green water – come and go
Like us from depth to height – suddenly seem
Translucent in the glancing lights that show
Where their quick-stirring forms are flickering.
We watch and hold each other's hands till evening,
And as we watch, our souls dart to and fro
Between the lights of speech and depths below,
The silent depths where touch is everything.

The Daily Planet

All day the noise of battle rolls,
The skirmishes and wars,
What peace or treaty can there be
Between two worlds like ours?

Could I be lost in Venus,
Could you be found in Mars,
Then I might search your tender wounds
And you my battle scars,
Then you might pull me from my sphere
Or fall to me from yours,
Were I, perchance, in Venus
And you, perhaps, in Mars.

What wary orbits we must keep
Around our dying sun,
Falling towards the verge of sleep
When all our wars are done,
Falling towards the verge of sleep
Where, lying side by side,
The angels of our planets weep
To see two worlds collide.

An Easter Triolet

We won't give up on love, it is a given
And given things can always live again.
The stone is rolled away, the rocks are riven
We won't give up on love, it is a given
The grave is made the very gate of heaven
We sowed in tears, but here's the golden grain:
We won't give up on love, it is a given
And here's a given thing that lives again.

Wedding Ring: four sonnets for Maggie

The Ring, 22.07.1984

Join hands with me and step into the ring
Shining in white with flowers in your hair.
The Word himself will give us songs to sing
And move the hidden voices of the air.
Here in his garden, where he laid his treasure
And came himself before the day was dawning,
Here where he gave a gift beyond our measure,
And Mary's footfall echoed in the morning,
Here he will raise us up and quench our thirst,
Setting upon our happiness his sign,
As, at his bidding in the wedding feast,
Waters of cleansing reddened into wine.
Then we shall turn to him with joy and sing
Whose love surrounds us in a golden ring.

Anniversary 22.07.2011

Again we celebrate our patroness
Who brings us both the news of resurrection,
Who finds the garden in the wilderness
And finds in love an unbroken connection,
As we did twenty-seven years ago,
Walking together through an open door
Into the garden where we both still grow,
Where making love is always making more;

More of my life is woven in with you
Than all the life I had before we met,
More to love and cherish, tried and true
Than ever there were sorrows to forget.
Therefore I bless the winter and the rain
For in His garden love is come again.

Dark Wind

All night a dark wind blows about our windows
And chases whispers through my dreaming head;
Dry voices sift and fall in ash and cinders,
In acrid conversation with the dead,
Whose ghosts go round in circles down from
    Heaven,
Whose ghosts go round in circles up from Hell,
Whose pace, within the strictest measure even,
Breaks in the drill and rhythm of a bell ...

Were I to wake alone I would be weeping
With shiftless sorrow, restless, rootless dread.
Instead I wake to warmth, to find you sleeping,
My living comfort, burrowed in our bed.
You reach across and still the drilling bell
And stretch and yawn and kiss me. All is well.

A Renewal of Vows

So, open up the treasure-casket, love,
The treasure is still there, the hidden things
That *love* contains; old words, like wedding rings,
Surround their mysteries. They live and move
As breath renews them, burnished as the gold
Around our fingers, glowing as we make
The vows that make us new again: *I take,*
Protect, and *comfort, cherish, have* and *hold,*
The same old words, that cannot stay the same
For they have grown, as we have, more than old,
They change and deepen like all things that live,
They compass more and still have more to give.
All that I have is yours, *all that I am*
I give again, with all I will become.

Be gentle with them, Memory

Be gentle with them, Memory,
My sad companions.
Give them your quiet fields and country walks,
Long nights of careful love
And sunlit mornings filled with idle talk,
With babbling of lovers.
Redeem them from all bitter words
And hurtful silences,
Recall my unpleased friends to amity.
And, Memory, at nightfall close their eyes
With tender breath and happy whispering,
With quiet laughter fluttering the dark.

Lapis Lazuli

For Felicity

I drop into your hands this drop of stone,
This lapidary lapis lazuli
Which will outlast my body breath and bone.
So when you wear it after, may it be
A hidden source of every azure blue,
A little sign of love in lightning skies,
A present that the past still gives to you,
A piece of heaven earthed, to match your eyes.

Prayer/Walk

A hidden path that starts at a dead end,
Old ways, renewed by walking with a friend,
And crossing places taken hand in hand,

The passages where nothing need be said,
With bruised and scented sweetness underfoot
And unexpected birdsong overhead,

The sleeping life beneath a dark-mouthed burrow,
The rooted secrets rustling in a hedgerow,
The land's long memory in ridge and furrow,

A track once beaten and now overgrown
With complex textures, every kind of green,
Land- and cloud-scape melting into one,

The rich meandering of streams at play,
A setting out to find oneself astray,
And coming home at dusk a different way.

Part III

Word and World

On being told my poetry was found in a broken photo-copier

My poetry is jamming your machine,
It broke the photo-copier, I'm to blame,
With pictures copied from a world unseen.

My poem is in the works – I'm on the scene –
We free my verse, and I confess my shame:
My poetry is jamming your machine.

Though you berate me with what might have been,
You stop to read the poem just the same,
And pictures copied from a world unseen,

Subvert the icons on your mental screen
And open windows with a whispered name;
My poetry is jamming your machine.

For chosen words can change the things they mean
And set the once-familiar world aflame
With pictures copied from a world unseen.

The mental props give way on which you lean,
The world you see will never be the same,
My poetry is jamming your machine
With pictures copied from a world unseen.

Spell

Summon the summoners, the twenty-six
Enchanters. Spelling silence into sound,
They bind and loose, they find and are not found.
Re-call the river-tongues from *Alph* to *Styx*.
Summon the summoners, the shaping shapes,
The grounds of sound, the generative *gramma*,
Signs of the Mystery, inscribed *arcana,*
Runes from the root-tree written in the deeps,
Leaves from the tale-tree lifted, swift and free,
Shining, re-combining in their dance
The genesis of every utterance,
Pattering the pattern of the Tree.
Summon the summoners, and let them sing.

The summoners will summon everything.

Hollows

I lift you lightly, you were made for me;
No box of rain to give the grateful dead,
But breath instead and beauty for the living.
A certain shaping of the mountain air
Censes its gentle wood-scent in your hollows.
The high, dry, hallows of Montana
First saw you braced and fretted, resonant
And ready to be sounded into song.
The smallest tremor trembles through your form
And turns the air to music. My full heart
Is poured into your forming emptiness
And given back as passion for another,
Your hollows hold a weight that sets me free,
I lift you lightly, you were made for me.

Muse

I stop and sense a subtle presence here,
An opalescent shimmer in the light,
And catch, just at the corner of my eye,
A shifting shape that no one else can see;
Just on the edge, the very edge of sight
Just where the air is brightening, and where
The sky is coloured underneath a cloud.
And so she comes to keep her tryst with me.
She comes with music, music faintly heard,
A trace, a grace-note, floating in clear air,
As over hidden springs the hazels stir.
Time quivers and then she is at my side;
A quickened breath, a feather-touch on skin,
A sudden swift connection, deep within.

Salvage

Perhaps this poem's just another write-off,
Another scrap of paper for the bin.
So, should I struggle on or turn the light off?

My muse, maybe, has booked another night off,
Without her help I can't even begin.
Perhaps this poem's just another write-off.

And yet I can't forget what I caught sight of;
A grace I mustn't lose, but cannot win,
So, should I struggle on, or turn the light off?

I'm darkened by the love I most make light of,
I cast aside what's not yet counted in.
Could I presume to recognise a write-off?

It is despair itself that I must fight off,
When giving up feels just like giving in,
So, should I struggle on, or turn the light off?

There's something here to salvage, something right
    off
Life's radar, or else underneath her skin.
Since I'm redeemed, (and I was once a write-off)
I'll struggle on until they turn the light off.

De Magistra

You were indeed my teacher, more than that,
Sole *Magistra* amidst the *Magisters*,
I conjured you that I might conjugate.
Summon me now, and the whole register
Of love and loving answers to your call.
I lift my lines like water from a well,
Spilling in sound, *amo amas amat*,
A *puer*'s poor libation at your feet.
My thankless muse, I meditate you now,
Your quick dark eyes still piercing my defence,
Your untouched hand touching the golden bough.
My mistress in the school of eloquence,
Strict arbitress of sentences and fines,
I asked for life, you gave me fourteen lines.

What if …

'But I say unto you, that every idle word that men
shall speak, they shall give account thereof in the day
of judgment. For by thy words thou shalt be justified,
and by thy words thou shalt be condemned.'
Matthew 12:36–37

What if every word we say
Never ends or fades away,
Gathers volume, gathers way,
Drums and dins us with dismay,
Surges on some dreadful day
When we cannot get away
Whelms us till we drown?

What if not a word is lost?
What if every word we cast;
Cruel, cunning, cold, accurst,
Every word we cut and paste,
Echoes to us from the past,
Fares and find us first and last,
Haunts and hunts us down?

What if every murmuration,
Every otiose oration,
Every blogger's obfuscation,
Every tweeted titivation
Every oath and imprecation,

Insidious insinuation,
Every verbal aberration,
Unexamined asservation,
Idiotic iteration,
Every facile explanation,
Drags us to the ground?

What if each polite evasion,
Every word of defamation,
Insults made by implication,
Querulous prevarication,
Compromise in convocation,
Propaganda for the nation,
False or flattering persuasion,
Blackmail and manipulation,
Simulated desperation
Grows to such reverberation
That it shakes our own foundation,
Shakes and brings us down?

Better that some words be lost,
Better that they should not last,
Tongues of fire and violence.
Word through whom the world is blessed,
Word in whom all words are graced,
Do not bring us to the test,
Give our clamant voices rest,
And the rest is silence.

The Cutting Edge

At my back, like you, I always hear
The edge, the cutting edge is coming near.

Not the blind fury
With the abhorred shears,
But this is what I fear:
The stealthy scissors of a blinded time
Cutting through accretions of the past
Dully and daily deleting whatever is not next,
Sneering and sniping and snipping,
Excising every sign-post from the text,
Paring all the parts that point away
To something other than our circled self.

I know the angels were the first to fall;
Cherub and Seraph spiralled down
In circling curlicues of sacred text,
Flaring in ink and paper to the floor,
The shredded evidence of our affair,
Our old, embarrassing affair with God.
And God himself will follow soon enough;
A little word so easy to excise,
Another snippet for the cutting room,
A sweeping on the heap of history.

But still at night I tiptoe to the door
To rustle through these severed strips of love,
And strew my heart with scraps of poetry,
Forbidden hopes and shards of mystery.
They rustle through me in my waking dreams
And so I'll have a heart-, a head-, a handful when
The scissors come for me.

For at my back, like you, I always hear
The cutting edge, the edge is coming near.

iOde

My private portal to a world between,
My placeless place of virtual exchange,
I see through you though you remain unseen
And make familiar what you once made strange.

You make a stranger means to make me 'friend'
Whom I can 'touch' to 'like', to show I care.
You make a means to every unknown end
And make one little screen an everywhere.

I am familiar with a hundred faces,
All famished for their fifteen minutes fame,
I am half present in a hundred places
But never present in the place I am.

I pull you from my pocket when you call,
I touch and swipe as I am bid to do,
You do my bidding too, you do it all,
What will you make of me, or I of you?

String Theory

For Girton choir

In the beginning,
only this,
a sound.

A sound
whose waves expand,
whose echoes still expend
themselves in riffs of time and space,
in overlapping amplitudes of bliss,
pattering into patterns, into persons, into us,
conscious harmonics, singing face to face.
Resounding into music now, we trace
in touches of a single string, our source,
flowing in everything, for everything
in the beginning, in the end,
is only this,
a sound.

Which Comes First, the Fish or the River?

For Michael Ward

Since every gift comes down from the all-giver,
How can we choose between the giver's gifts,
Or say which should come first, the fish or river?

He scatters first, and then calls us to gather,
To float upon his love our loving craft,
And sail our songs upstream, back to the giver.

He gives his gifts when we are met together,
Not in our splits, our schisms, and our rifts;
We cannot prize the fish and not the river,

Divide the two and say 'which would you rather?'
We drift through time on fragile little rafts
But time and life alike flow from the giver.

Away upstream, it all flows from the Father.
The stream is his own Spirit, giving gifts,
His Son, our brother, joins us in the river.

He is a *both-and* God, not *or,* or *either*
He gives full measure; steady, heady draughts!
The giver must come first, always the giver,
And we receive his gifts: both fish and river.

Imagine

A found sonnet from The Abolition of Man *by*
C.S. Lewis

Imagine a new natural philosophy;
I hardly know what I am asking for;
Far-off echoes, that primeval sense,
With blood and sap, Man's pre-historic piety,
Continually conscious, continually ...
Alive, alive and growing like a tree
And trees as dryads, or as beautiful,
The bleeding trees in Virgil and in Spenser
The tree of knowledge and the tree of life
Growing together, that great ritual
Pattern of nature, beauties branching out
The cosmic order, ceremonial,
Regenerate science, seeing from within ...

To participate is to be truly human.

Part IV

Intimations of Mortality

Holding and Letting Go

We have a call to live, and oh
A common call to die.
I watched you and my father go
To bid a friend goodbye.
I watched you hold my father's hand,
How could it not be so?
The gentleness of holding on
Helps in the letting go.

For when we feel our frailty
How can we not respond?
And reach to hold another's hand
And feel the common bond?
For then we touch the heights above
And every depth below,
We touch the very quick of love;
Holding and letting go.

Table Talk

'As thick as two short planks' is what you think,
But I'll be here when you are in your grave,
I'll hold the baked meats, you'll have me to thank.
It goes against my grain to hear you grieve
For all that's done and dusted. I am dumb,
But quarter-sawn and solid, the real deal,
Where you once wrote *mensa mensa mensam*,
And thought that writing made you the more real.

The day you die they'll cover me with cloth
That leaves me, as they leave you, in the dark
With all my scars and scratches underneath.
So clear me now and settle down to work.
Lean on me poet, till the lights go out:
I lie just under everything you write.

Never

Closing my eyes against all that is left to see,
Folding my hands when there's so much undone,
This is the last of the days that are left to me,
Last of the light and the warmth of the sun.

Hardly a moment it seems I have lived with you,
Swiftly I leave what has scarcely begun,
Telling again all I know I will never do,
Losing at last what has hardly been won.

Never to run through a resinous glade again,
Never to bathe in a clear-running stream,
Never to move between sunlight and shade again,
Never to wake or to sleep or to dream,

Never to look on the light of your face again,
Never to turn at the sound of your voice,
Never to yearn for your warmth and embrace again,
Dead to all feeling, desire or choice,

Never to love again, never to leave again,
Never to sing again, never to sigh,
Never to give again, never to grieve again,
Never to die again, never to die.

Worry Beads

I told them through the cold of January,
My hands half-frozen, feeling for their nubbed
And sliding touch, word-beads that rubbed
Against each other; I am not to worry
I am not to worry, till the tale is done.
Pick them up. Keep writing. Six a.m.:
Each black bead holds a tiny candle-flame
Repeated in the whisky-light of dawn.

I hear their voices and the touch of wood
On wood between their fingers in the sharp
Hellenic sunlight. Passion, fear, and hope
Passing away and coming to no good.
I will transcribe the pattern that they sound
As each dark bead comes slowly clicking down.

In Absentia

Now all I have's a map.
I follow lanes we never walked,
Unravelling the travelled lines
Where footpaths find the folds.

Unmappable, the moments I have missed,
All the terrain in you I never touched.
There is no bounding line that can contain,
No border that can circumscribe this absence
My terra firma, and my terra incognita.

Compass

The child they whirled around for blind man's bluff
Is spinning still within me, calling out
And feeling for the touch of hands that ease
And tease with disappearance from his world
Leaving him all at sea.

                             I feel for you,
Even in darkness I can sense you here.
My spinning child becomes a compass card
That turns and veers whichever way I steer.
What is it pulls the needle back to you?
A lapsing pattern of collapsing waves,
A flux, a pulse between two frozen poles
That we would not have chosen. Something nets
Me, heart and head, in hidden lines, directs
These strange migrations of my mind,
Takes bearings on a loss I cannot bear.

These words are like a scatter of black filings
Tracing the lines of force beneath this paper
Where you still hold the magnet; memory
In shreds again for you to reconfigure;
A disturbance in the field that puts me out
Of reckoning, and compass altogether.

My Inheritance

You left your little ship to me,
My hand is on her tiller now.
Before we parted, out at sea
You left your little ship to me.
Sharp shoals are showing on her lee,
And waves are breaking on her prow.
You left your little ship to me,
My hand is on her tiller now.

Pour out the Wine

Pour out the wine for one last glass with me
And praise with me the rooted fruitful vine.
Raise up the glass, give thanks for all you see,
Pour out the wine.

Sweeten my time whilst I can call it mine;
The axe is laid already to the tree
And all we raise aloft must soon decline.

So now, whilst hands can touch and eyes can see,
Raise up the glass and let your glance meet mine,
And when I'm gone, do this one thing for me,
Pour out the wine.

Part V

Clouds of Witness

Sonnets for the Saints

Columba

You called me and I came to Colmcille
To learn at last the meaning of my name,
Though you yourself were called, and not the caller.
He called through you and when He called I came,
Came to the edge at last, in Donegal,
Where bonfires burned and music lit the flame,
As from the shore I glimpsed that ragged sail
The Spirit filled to drive you from your home,
A fierce dove racing in a fiercer gale,
A swift wing flashing between sea and sky.
And with that glimpse I knew that I would fly
And find you out and serve you for a season,
My heaven hidden like your native isle,
Though somehow glimmering on each horizon.

Benedict

You sought to start a simple school of prayer,
A modest, gentle, moderate attempt,
With nothing made too harsh or hard to bear,
No treating or retreating with contempt,
A little rule, a small obedience
That sets aside, and tills the chosen ground,
Fruitful humility, chosen innocence,
A binding by which freedom might be found.

You call us all to live, and see good days,
Centre in Christ and enter in his peace,
To seek his Way amidst our many ways,
Find blessedness in blessing, peace in praise,
To clear and keep for Love a sacred space
That we might be beginners in God's grace.

Augustine of Canterbury

'Oh loving Lord don't send me to the English,
Boorish and brutal pagans that they are.'
You prayed, you wrote to Gregory in anguish,
But he replied: 'Since you have come so far,
Your hand is on the plough, you must continue,
And reach them on their rain-drenched island shore.
There's something in the English that will win you
And Christ himself will open up the door.'

And so the gospel came to Canterbury,
The very gospel book we still possess,
Weathering the storms of history
In all its splendour and its hiddenness.
We bless you for that gospel you proclaim,
Bless your successors as they do the same.

Cuddy

Cuthbertus says the dark stone up in Durham
Where I have come on pilgrimage to pray.
But not this great cathedral, nor the solemn
Weight of Norman masonry we lay
Upon your bones could hold your soul in prison.
Free as the Cuddy ducks they named for you,
Loosed by the lord who died to pay your ransom,
You roam the North just as you used to do;
Always on foot and walking with the poor,
Breaking the bread of angels in your cave,
A sanctuary, a sign, an open door,
You follow Christ through keening wind and wave,
To be and bear with him where all is borne;
The heart of heaven, in your Inner Farne.

Hilda of Whitby

Called to a conflict and a clash of cultures,
Where insults flew whilst synod was in session,
You had the gift to find the gift in others,
A woman's wisdom, deftness and discretion.
You made a space and place for poetry
When outcast Caedmon, crouching in the byre,
Was called by grace into community
And local language joined the Latin choir.

Abbess we need your help, we need your wisdom,
Your strong recourse to reconciliation,
Your power tempered by God's hidden kingdom,
Your exercise of true imagination.
Pray for our synods now, princess of peace,
That every fettered gift may find release.

Bede

Above Bede's tomb in Durham Cathedral one of his
prayers is written in gold. It reads:

> *Christus est stella matutina, Alleluia*
> *Qui nocte saeculi transacta, Alleluia*
> *Lucem vitae sanctis promittit, Alleluia;*
> *Et pandit aeternam, Alleluia*

> (Christ is the morning star
> Who when the night of this world is past
> Brings to his saints the promise of the light of life
> And opens everlasting day.)

I kneel above your bones and read your words;
Church-Latin letters, shimmering in gold,
A kingdom-glimmer through the dark and cold,
A revelation gleaming on the shards
Of all our broken lives and promises.
Christus est stella matutina
Qui nocte saeculi transacta
Christ is the morning star. He promises
The light of life when this dark night is past...
Lucem vitae sanctis promittit
You speak for all His wounded witnesses:
The morning star will shine on us at last.
Scholar and saint, illuminate the way
That opens into everlasting day.

Hildegard of Bingen

A feather on the breath of God at play,
You saw the play of God in all creation.
You drew eternal light into each day,
And every living breath was inspiration.
You made a play with every virtue playing,
Made music for each sister-soul to sing,
Listened for what each herb and stone was saying,
And heard the Word of God in everything.

Mother from mother earth and Magistra,
Your song revealed God's hidden gift to us;
The verdant fire, his holy harbinger
The greening glory of *viriditas*.
'Cherish this earth that keeps us all alive'
Either we hear you, or we don't survive.

Francis

'Francis rebuild my church which, as you see
Is falling into ruin.' From the cross
Your saviour spoke to you and speaks to us
Again through you. Undoing set you free,
Loosened the traps of trappings, cast away
The trammelling of all that costly cloth
We wind our saviour in. At break of day
He set aside his grave-clothes. Your new birth
Came like a daybreak too. Naked and true
To poverty and to the gospel call,
You woke to Christ and Christ awoke in you
And set to work through all your love and skill
To make our ruin good, to bless and heal,
To wake the Christ in us and make us whole.

Clare

Santa Chiara, lovely claritas
Whose soul in stillness holds love's pure reflection,
Shining through you as Holy Caritas,
Lucid and lucent, bringing to perfection
The girl whom Love has called to call us all
Back into truth, simplicity and grace.
Your love for Francis, radiant through the veil,
Reveals in both of you your saviour's face.
Christ holds the mirror of your given life
Up to the world he gives himself to save,
A sacrament to keep your city safe,
A window into his eternal love.
Unveiled in heaven, dancing in the light,
Pray for this pilgrim soul in his dark night.

Julian of Norwich

Show me O anchoress, your anchor-hold
Deep in the love of God, and hold me fast,
Show me again in whose hands we are held,
Speak to me from your window in the past,
Tell me again the tale of Love's compassion
For all of us who fall onto the mire,
How he is wounded with us, how his passion
Quickens the love that haunted our desire.
Show me again the wonder of at-one-ment
Of Christ-in-us distinct and yet the same,
Who makes, and loves, and keeps us in each
      moment,
And looks on us with pity not with blame.
Keep telling me, for all my faith may waver,
Love is his meaning, only love, forever.

Latimer

Latimer's pulpit, you can touch the wood,
Sound for yourself the syllables of grace
That sounded and resounded through this place;
A quickened word, a kindling for good
In evil times; when malice held the cards
And played them, in the play of politics,
When knaves with knives were taking all the tricks,
When Christendom was shivered into shards,
When King and Queen were pitched in different
    camps,
When burning books could stoke the fire for men,
When such were stacked against him – even then
Latimer knew that hearts alone are trumps.
He gave the King of Hearts his proper name,
He touched this wood, and kindled love to flame.

George Herbert

Gentle exemplar, help us in our trials
With all that passed between you and your Lord,
That intimate exchange of frowns and smiles
Which chronicled your love-match with the Word.
Your manuscript, entrusted to a friend,
Has been entrusted now to every soul,
We make a new beginning in your end
And find your broken heart has made us whole.
Time has transplanted you, and you take root,
Past changing in the paradise of Love.
Help me to trace your Temple, tune your lute,
And listen for an echo from above.
Open the window, let me hear you sing,
And see the Word with you in everything.

Lancelot Andrewes

Your mind is fixed upon the sacred page,
A candle lights your study through the night,
The choicest wit, the scholar of the age,
Seeking the light in which we see the light.
Grace concentrates in you, your hand is firm,
Tracing the line of truth in all its ways.
Through you the great translation finds its form,
'And still there are not tongues enough to praise.'
Your day began with uttering his name
And when you close your eyes you rest in him,
His constant star still draws you to your home,
Our chosen *stella praedicantium*.
You set us with the Magi on the Way
And shine in Christ unto the rising day.

Samuel Taylor Coleridge

'Stop, Christian passer-by!—Stop, child of God!'
You made your epitaph imperative,
And stopped this wedding guest! But I am glad
To stop with you and start again, to live
From that pure source, the all-renewing stream,
Whose living power is imagination,
And know myself a child of the I AM,
Open and loving to his whole creation.

Your glittering eye taught mine to pierce the veil,
To let his light transfigure all my seeing,
To serve the shaping Spirit whom I feel,
And make with him the poem of my being.
I follow where you sail towards our haven,
Your wide wake lit with glimmerings of heaven.

C.S. Lewis

From 'beer and Beowulf' to the seven heavens,
Whose music you conduct from sphere to sphere,
You are our portal to those hidden havens
Whence we return to bless our being here.
Scribe of the Kingdom, keeper of the door
Which opens onto all we might have lost,
Ward of a word-hoard in the deep heart's core,
Telling the tale of Love from first to last.
Generous, capacious, open, free,
Your wardrobe-mind has furnished us with worlds
Through which to travel, whence we learn to see
Along the beam, and hear at last the heralds
Sounding their summons, through the stars that
    sing,
Whose call at sunrise brings us to our King.

The Two Kings: A meditation on
Thomas Cranmer

'Soon after he had signed the fifth recantation he
had a dream in which he saw two kings contending
together for his soul. One of the kings was Jesus and
the other was Henry VIII.' *Thomas Cranmer, Jasper
Ridley (Oxford, 1962, p. 399)*

Bearing a light to break the gloom
That gathers in his littered room,
After the Latin mass is sung,
Cranmer essays the English tongue.
Before his straining eyes is set
The single word *Magnificat*.
He writes, delighting in the word,
My soul doth magnify the Lord.

Elsewhere other voices sing
To laud and magnify the king;
A woman turns her whitened face
To beg his majesty for grace
And offers up her perjured soul
A sacrifice to bluff King Hal
Whose chains and scourges still disclose
The blood within the Tudor rose.

Could Cranmer ever hope to bruise
That hydra-headed serpent, whose
Insinuating influence
Turned in the word *obedience*,
And tempted him, upon his knees,
To tender Caesar Peter's keys?
He offered Henry heaven's trust,
Dust bowing down to worship dust.

Yet he, whom Satan had convinced
To put his trust in such a prince
And so provoke his jealous God,
Denying the redeeming blood,
Was chosen, judged, and justified,
In the same blood that he denied.
So Cranmer, who betrayed the Lord,
Was brought to glory through his Word

As, through the medium of a dream,
The Word in him redeemed the time.
His faith, denied and found again,
Held fast in that foul Oxford rain
Where, chained and bound by pious friars,
He thrust his right hand in their fires
And crying out in fits and starts
Burnt his best sermon on their hearts.

Patterns (Tree and Leaf)

Tolkien is leaning back into an oak
Old, gnarled, distinct in bole and burr
As, from the burr and bowl of his old pipe,
Packed with tightly patterned shreds of leaf,
The smoke ascends in rings and wreathes of air
To catch the autumn light and meet such leaves
As circle through its wreathes and patter down
In patterns of their own to the rich ground.

Again he contemplates the tree of tales:
The roots of language and its rings of growth,
'The tongue and tale and teller all coeval'
And he becomes a pattern making patterns,
A tale telling tales and turning leaves,
From the print of thumb and finger on his pipe
To the print and press and pattern of his books
And all their prints and imprints in our minds,
Out to this grainy patterned photograph
Of 'Tolkien, leaning back into an oak'.

We coin the hollows of your beaten face

We coin the hollows of your beaten face
And hang your agony in hall-marked silver,
Display in church your prosperous embrace,
Fast in the golden cross a diamond splinter.

We must efface your crucified reproach,
Betrayed by pains beyond our sympathy;
Your agony has cast beyond your reach
A world beyond the reach of agony.
Christ, we must make you distant, splendid, rich,
We cannot live with your humanity.

We Stand to Prayer

The splendour of Nirvana is not ours,
We have no middle eye, no mystic wings,
And our brief visions take us unawares.
We stand to prayer as rows of earthen jars
Whose dark mouths open onto hidden things:
A secret kingdom where the poor are kings.
Here is an image of that inner place,
The quiet mountain country of the soul
With silver pools where lions drink their fill
And the pale unicorns lie down in peace.
Here is an emblem of the hidden grace
Beneath the flux and turmoil of what happens,
A quiet kingdom where the silence deepens,
Whose heart is hallowed by the Prince of Peace.

Descent

They sought to soar into the skies,
Those classic gods of high renown,
For lofty pride aspires to rise,
But you came down.

You dropped down from the mountains sheer,
Forsook the eagle for the dove,
The other gods demanded fear,
But you gave love.

Where chiselled marble seemed to freeze
Their abstract and perfected form,
Compassion brought you to your knees,
Your blood was warm.

They called for blood in sacrifice,
Their victims on an altar bled,
When no one else could pay the price,
You died instead.

They towered above our mortal plain,
Dismissed this restless flesh with scorn,
Aloof from birth and death and pain,
But you were born.

Born to these burdens, borne by all
Born with us all 'astride the grave',
Weak, to be with us when we fall,
And strong to save.

Part VI

Three Sequences

Canon C.26.1

'Every Bishop, Priest, or Deacon, is under obligation,
not being let by sickness or some other urgent cause,
to say daily the morning and evening prayers, either
privately or openly.' *Canon Law*

'The faith and the hope and the love are all in the
waiting.' *T.S. Eliot*

1.

Walk into the darkness, sit and wait.
Wait for the God who takes your breath away
And withers all your roots. Look at your feet
In silence till he gives you words to pray,
Or breaks your heart and turns the other way
And there is nothing left to do but wait.
Wait for the God who sends the promised rain
And drowns his people, gives the living bread
And starves them, who is tender to the pain
He causes as he severs heart and head,
Destroys the living and revives the dead,
Exalts with loss and crucifies with gain.
Observe his wound: you cannot staunch the blood
That seeps and darkens through the patient wood.

2.

My spine is rooted in the patient wood,
Seated in darkness, breathing out for prayer,
Meditating the primeval flood.
The dark waters of the Lord's despair
Still hold aloft the wood, the grain, the blood,
The lost ark cast away like wasted bread
Upon the waters. Coming up for air
I count my breath and watch a distant fire,
A sanctuary candle's tiny star,
An icon's faded cross and haloed head.
I turn again towards the quiet wood
Rooted in darkness and exhale. My prayer
Ghosts like a raven over the grey flood
Calling upon its maker to be fed.

3.

I count my breath and watch a distant fire,
A doubtful image, which it hardly lights,
An icon's batwing shadows in the flare
Flung to the walls and fluttered to the roof.
Watch-light, wick-light, dawn-light casting lots
Which should succeed, with taken breath, the brief
Seconds as they slip away. Enough
Light for the present grief, and just enough
To see beyond the candle-flame His head
Upon a cross and in His hands a book
Open and illegible. The dead
Strokes dark and cold however hard I look.
This shadowed light is not enough. I wait
A Fiat Lux which will make sense of it.

4.

Wait for the voice and calling of the bell
To break his silence, for a greater light
To flood his darkness. Feel what you must feel;
The pressure of your body and the slight
Stretch and tension of familiar fear,
Weighting the consequence of every choice.
You hear the voices that you choose to hear
But never, in your heart, your own voice.
Your silence seethes with whispering. Your eyes
Light on the icon. Nothing will make sense
Of love and suffering, these are mysteries
Buried beneath your own experience,
Innocents praying nightly for release.
Wait for the day when you will see them rise.

5.

Turn back into the darkness of the wood
And breathe again, till he inspires the dead
Letters of his open book with life
And kindles flames of purpose in your grief
By whose fierce light the letters may be read;
Words for the silent Word himself to speak
Before the cross, above the open book,
Read them aloud and wait till they are true.
Out of the past and over the grey flood,
Within the wood and through the welling blood,
The jubilation of his hidden voice,
Redeeming all the loss it echoes through,
Cries from the lowest pit of Hell: 'Rejoice!
You have not chosen me but I have chosen you.'

Six Glimpses

1. Steam

He's old enough, just, to remember steam.
He's heard the sound of shunting in a station,
The hiss of steam released, the sudden scream
Of the steam whistle, felt the sense of danger,
Of hidden heat and power, enormous shapes
Looming from darkness where their nameplates
    gleam.

It's all nostalgia now, all just a gleam
In an ad-man's eye, the 'bygone age of steam',
Engines with faces, kiddies' cut-out shapes,
'Thomas and friends' all cosy in the station.
But when he dreams it, he still dreams of danger,
Of crushing speed and weight. He tries to scream

Before it runs him down. He cannot scream
But must endure the impact till the gleam
Of morning finds and rescues him from danger
And he breathes again. Thin wisps of steam
Drift from the kettle. From the Classic station
A Bach cantata builds fantastic shapes

Inside his waking mind. The music shapes
His mood whilst driving till the distant scream
And choke of traffic fades. He finds the Station.
The franchised coffee counters gadgets gleam.
He sits there killing time, the windows steam.
He's trying not to think about the danger

In all these brief encounters, yet its danger
That still draws him, as he draws the shapes
Of his desires dancing in the steam.
The way he lives just makes him want to scream,
But still he lives and lives just for the gleam
That gilds the ones who meet him at the station.

They read each other's eyes and leave the station
Tremulous, oblivious of danger,
Walking together through the rain, the gleam
Reflected from their raincoats, two dark shapes
Headed for that tunnel where a scream
Can sound at last in heat and noise and steam.

We follow the gleam: desire fuels and shapes
Our lives with danger, till there comes a scream
Of brakes, a station, and we vanish like steam.

2. Rain

She's tried the handle but she can't get in.
Locked out again, she's pouring out her love
By cradling her dolly in the rain
With the deep concentration of a child,
Giving the doll what she was never given,
Complete attention and a gentle touch.

The social services have been in touch.
They say they called but found nobody in.
Reports will have been filed, that is a given,
(The missing word in those reports is love)
Reports about the welfare of the child,
Who whispers to her dolly in the rain,

Whose stepfather is stumbling through the rain,
His pit of anger still too hot to touch,
A rage that started in him as a child,
And broke the man whose life is breaking in
And kicking down four-letter words like love
And paying people out. Nothing is given,

Everything comes at a terrible price. Given
A chance, things might be different. Still rain,
Cold and indifferent, quenched his little love,
But not his rage and pain, raw to the touch.
He fumbles with his key and staggers in
Followed by the cold and trembling child.

His target is the mother of the child,
Resenting her for all that she has given
And he cannot repay. He closes in
With savage blows under the drumming rain,
Crushing the flesh that once he loved to touch,
Hammering down a coffin lid on love.

What will survive of us, they say, is love.
The one survivor here is a lost child,
Soothing her dolly with a tender touch,
Remembering the day that it was given,
Listening to the drumming of the rain.
When the police arrive she lets them in.

They leave the dead untouched, and unforgiven,
Wrap up the child and drive her through the rain.
'I love you,' she still whispers, 'let me in.'

3. Fire

He cannot stop these memories of fire
Crackling and flashing in his head.
Not just in fevered dreams; the fires break
Into the light of day. He burns with shame,
But still he screams and shakes, because the dead,
Are burning too and screaming out his name.

They told him his condition had a name,
But words can't quench the memory of fire,
Nor can they ever resurrect the dead.
They told him it was 'all inside his head',
That post-traumatic stress need cause no shame.
The army gave him time for a short break.

But that's what he's afraid of. He will break
And break forever; lose his life and name,
Shake like a child who's sickening with shame,
He who had been 'courageous under fire'
Who always stemmed the panic, kept his head.
And now all night he wishes he were dead

And cannot die. Instead he sees the dead
In all their last contortions. Bodies break
Under his wheels, a child's severed head
Amidst the rubble seems to call his name
Over the clattering of rifle fire,
Stuttering guns that shake with him in shame.

He's left his family. 'Oh it's a shame',
The neighbours said, 'That marriage was long dead
– You can't live with a man who's shouting "Fire!"
All night like that. His kids needed a break,
And in the end she had to change her name.'
'They'll never fix what's wrong inside his head.'

'Some people seem to cope and get ahead,
The army makes them better men, a shame
He couldn't cope.' Now he has lost his name
And his address. He only knows the dead.
He sleeps on benches but they come and break
His sleep. They keep him under constant fire.

And come November, when they name the dead,
He waits in silence for his heart to break
And every poppy burns with hopeless fire.

4. Earth

Here at the graveside, holding onto earth,
The time approaches when he will let go.
But now his freezing fist is clenched as hard
As ice around the dirt of which we're made
And his poor heart is ice beneath the floe
Waiting for the moment of release.

The priest has told him that he should release
The earth he holds when he hears *earth to earth*
And *dust to dust* 'but just go with the flow'
He said and smiled. Instead he wants to go
A million miles from here. Why were we made
For pain like this? The flinty ground is hard

And all their breath is frosted. Frosted hard.
The tears that cannot melt for their release
Wait in their frozen channels. We're unmade
By one another's deaths. We go to earth
Like animals at bay. Words come and go
But we are hiding deep beneath their flow.

So with this liturgy, its surge and flow
Seem so remote and dreamlike that it's hard
To concentrate, remember to let go
His handful of poor soil, and release
Its rattle at the coffin lid as *earth*
To earth... remembereth whereof we are made ...

Sounds out in tones and undertones all made
Unreal, ethereal, by the easy flow
Of practised piety. Only the earth
Is silent as his heart, silent and hard
Because no words will do. 'Oh just release
Us into silence, finish. Let us go.'

At last it's over and he turns to go
Back to the empty house, the bed unmade,
Cards and condolences, a press release
About the accident, bereavement leaflets, flow
Over the floor. He reads: *it's always hard …
You may be tempted just to go to earth …*

Only at midnight dreams release the flow
Of frozen tears. Memory melts the hard
Heart last, and let's love go to the good earth.

5. Air

She always liked to be in the fresh air,
Outdoors and in the open. She felt best
Striding ahead. She always took the lead,
So full of confidence. And that last night
She set off happily. We said 'take care'.
How can someone simply disappear?

We waited, worried, for her to appear,
Maybe she'd just stayed out to take the air,
She'd phone if she was late, she knows we care.
We tried hard not to panic, did our best,
Phoned the police at midnight and all night
Paced the house shaking, but they had no lead.

Next day they combed the woods for some small
    lead
They told us that when children disappear
They sometimes stay with friends for just a night,
But they could hardly fake that casual air.
'We'll find her soon you know, we'll do our best.'
And all the world goes by without a care.

We go through everything again; how we took care,
We retrace every step. We take the lead
In each pretending we hope for the best,
And watch each flimsy hope just disappear.
Panic returns. We're gulping drafts of air,
Flailing through that dreadful second night.

The days you get through but it's worst at night,
Your mind goes round in circles. You don't care
What time it is, you swallow empty air
And sweat and shiver. The slow minutes lead
Each other round the clock and disappear.
No one knows what to do, or what is best.

They call the search off. They have done their best.
There was no trace of anything that night,
And any clues are bound to disappear.
The media make an offer (do they care?)
A special broadcast might produce a lead
'When the red light is on you're live on air.'

Love, if you're listening, oh please take care
Call us ... call anyone ... the smallest lead ...
Our small words hit the wall in the dead air.

6. Prayer

She lights a candle, deepens into prayer;
The unprayed images of day receive
Complete attention as she opens them
With love, letting the Spirit search the depths
Of those dark things she glimpses through the day;
She brings them to the wounds of one who heals.

Desire is a wound that never heals
It seems to her. And she begins her prayer
With that glimpse in the station, a grey day,
A brief encounter. May that man receive
Protection in his dangers and his depths,
He and his friend, Oh Christ *remember them*.

That child with the Police, *remember them*.
Is Heaven deaf? Where is the Love that heals
A girl glimpsed through the rain? Who knows the
    depths
Of that bewildered gaze? She cries in prayer,
Cries with the crying child; may she receive
Protection, comfort, sleep, at close of day.

Remember them. It is Remembrance Day–
–The War Memorial, *we will remember them*
That shaking man she'd glimpsed, let him receive
Some strong touch of the wounded love that heals
For he seemed all on fire. Now in her prayer
She calls the quenching fountain from its depths.

And then that frozen funeral ... the depths
Of grief she knows only too well. The day
Had turned so dark and wintry and her prayer
Rises on frosted breath. *Remember them*
And reach a cold man with the warmth that heals.
May he so let love go as to receive.

Open our clenched fists Heaven, to receive
The touch of mercy, mercy in the depths.
Open your wound in us, the wound that heals ...
And that sad broadcast at the close of day
Those parents, their lost girl, *remember them*
Gather these tears and turn them into prayer ...

All night she turns the images of day
Into insistent prayer, *Remember them*
Remember them, and lift them into Prayer.

On Reading the *Commedia*

'The reading of Dante is not merely a pleasure, a *tour de force*, or a lesson; it is a vigorous discipline for the heart, the intellect, the whole man.' **Gladstone**, *Anne Isba (Boydell & Brewer, 2006, p. 13)*

Inferno

1. In Medias Res

And so I start again, here in the middle,
The middle of a life I scarcely know.
How many guesses left to get the riddle?

The woods are dark and darker shadows grow.
I followed someone here, but lost her leading,
With nothing but my lostness left to show.

The voice that drew me on is faint and fading,
But something else is creeping up behind,
Over whose heart, I wonder, are we treading?

My shadow-beasts can scent, though they are blind,
All three are here, the leopard, lion, wolf,
My kith and kin, the emblems of my kind.

They've come to draw me back across the gulf,
Back from the path I wanted to have chosen.
Fall back, they call, *you can't run from yourself,*

Fall to the place where every hope is frozen...
But not this time. This time I choose to choose
The other path, path of the dead and risen,

To try the hidden heart of things, to let go, lose,
To lose myself and find again the voice
That called and drew me here, my freeing muse.

Begin again she calls, *you have the choice,*
Little by little, you can travel far,
Learn to lament before you can rejoice,

Sing to the shadows, sing and do not fear
But sing them into love little by little.
Begin the song exactly where you are.

And so I start again here in the middle.

2. Through the Gate

Begin the song exactly where you are,
For where you are contains where you have been
And holds the vision of your final sphere.

And do not fear the memory of sin:
There is a light that heals, and, where it falls,
Transfigures and redeems the darkest stain

Into translucent colour. Loose the veils
And draw the curtains back, unbar the doors
Of that dread threshold where your spirit fails,

The hopeless gate that holds in all the fears
That haunt your shadowed city, fling it wide
And open to the light that finds, and fares

Through the dark pathways where you run and
    hide,
Through all the alleys of your riddled heart,
As pierced and open as his wounded side.

Open the map to him and make a start,
And down the dizzy spirals, through the dark,
His light will go before you. Let him chart

And name and heal. Expose the hidden ache
To him, the stinging fires and smoke that blind
Your judgement, carry you away, the mirk

And muted gloom in which you cannot find
The love that you once thought worth dying for.
Call him to all you cannot call to mind.

He comes to harrow Hell and now to your
Well-guarded fortress let his love descend.
The icy ego at your frozen core

Can hear his call at last. Will you respond?

3. Vexilla Regis

I hear his call, now help me to respond,
My freeing muse. I need your presence here,
For poetry alone moves me beyond

The known and over-known, beyond the sheer
Drop into darkness and the all-unknown
To the last limits and the true frontier,

Where light and life dare to begin again.
Reason alone will never take me there,
The shaping spirit of imagination

Must also be my guide and bring me where
We pass the centre, turn the world around
And find the first steps of the hidden stair

That climbs out of these pits, far underground,
Against the stream of Lethe. Help me climb
Out of the depths that you have helped me sound.

Little by little, one step at a time
Towards the other side, the star-lit world
Where he has gone before and for all time.

The world-tree's steadfast roots are crossed and
    coiled,
But on the tree of life he dies for me.
Vexilla Regis sounds and all unfurled

The royal banners of the true and free
Stream out against the tempest and the fear
And summon me to all that I should be.

Up from that black and smothered atmosphere
I toil towards the light. The worst is past.
I hear the voice that called me, deep and clear

And let Love draw me into light at last.

Purgatorio

1. De Magistro

I thank my God I have emerged at last,
Blinking from Hell, to see these quiet stars,
Bewildered by the shadows that I cast.

You set me on this stair, in those rich hours
Pacing your study, chanting poetry.
The Word in you revealed his quickening powers,

Removed the daily veil, and let me see,
As sunlight played along your book-lined walls,
That words are windows onto mystery.

From Eden, whence the living fountain falls
In music, from the tower of ivory,
And from the hidden heart, he calls

In the language of Adam, creating memory
Of unfallen speech. He sets creation
Free from the carapace of history.

His image in us is imagination,
His Spirit is a sacrifice of breath
Upon the letters of his revelation.

In mid-most of the word-wood is a path
That leads back to the springs of truth in speech.
You showed it to me, kneeling on your hearth,

You showed me how my halting words might reach
To the mind's maker, to the source of Love,
And so you taught me what it means to teach.

Teaching, I have my ardours now to prove,
Climbing with joy the steps of Purgatory.
Teacher and pupil, both are on the move,

As fellow pilgrims on a needful journey.

2. Love in Idleness

When I am bogged in indolence again
It's purgatory for me, as for Belacqua,
Hanging around instead of getting on

With his salvation. I can't lift a finger.
The snow is falling heavily outside.
The earth gets lighter as the sky gets darker.

I shiver where I'm sitting (window wide
For snow-flakes to drop in and fade away)
And hide myself in something else's hide.

Coat panther-black and shabby hat wolf-grey,
As my numb fingers wrap about my pen,
All I need is fire and something to say.

Belacqua's lute speaks with the tongues of men,
The tongue-tied mind is loosened into praise.
I slip the disc back in its sleeve again:

One side is columns stiff with turgid prose
About the quattrocento, on the other
A sound-box holds the craftsman's fretted rose

With Florence in the background. What a cover
For the God who spoke through someone else's
   fingers
When ours were still entwined with one another.

Ages ago we heard the music linger
Before this light had lost its radiance,
And cast on love the shadow of our hunger;

We spoke of free will and of innocence
And trod the pavements of the fourth cornice
Where love is to be purged of indolence.

I write these verses pending my release.

3. Dancing Through The Fire

'per te poeta fui, per te Christiano' (Purg. 22:73)

Then stir my love in idleness to flame
To find at last the free refining fire
That guards the hidden garden whence I came.

O do not kill, but quicken my desire:
Better to spur me on than leave me cold.
Not maimed I come to you, I come entire,

Lit by the loves that warm, the lusts that scald,
That you may prove the one, reprove the other,
Though both have been the strength by which I
   scaled

The steps so far to come where poets gather
And sing such songs as love gives them to sing.
I thank God for the ones who brought me hither

And taught me by example how to bring
The slow growth of a poem to fruition
And let it be itself, a living thing,

Taught me to trust the gifts of intuition
And still to try the tautness of each line,
Taught me to taste the grace of transformation

And trace in dust the face of the divine,
Taught me the truth, as poet and as Christian,
That drawing water turns it into wine.

Now I am drawn through their imagination
To dare to dance with them into the fire,
Harder than any grand renunciation,

To bring to Christ the heart of my desire
Just as it is in every imperfection,
Surrendered to his bright refiner's fire

That love might have its death and resurrection.

Paradiso

1. Look Up

Look up at the resplendent lights of heaven
In all the glory of their otherness,
Within you and beyond you, simply given!

Let go your grandeur, love your littleness,
Begin a journey into clarity
And find again the love in loveliness,

The constant love in your inconstancy.
Reflected light you're not yet fit to bear,
Pearlescent preface to eternity,

She glimmers through the veils you make her wear,
Delights and glories in each difference,
In every variation everywhere.

Now let love raise and ravish every sense,
Quicksilver scatterings of consciousness,
She makes you myriad-minded, you can dance

In her swift sway and swing, the suddenness
Of ecstasy, third heaven's heady swirl,
That lifts and flings her lovers into bliss.

Remember tenderly you glimpsed a girl
Whose smile transfigured all without her knowing.
The tangles of your loving here unfurl

And find their freedom, every knot undoing,
Mistakes unmade, and unkind words unsaid,
The spring released at last and freely flowing,

As freely you forgive yourselves. The seed
Of love, long-planted, breathes and blossoms here
Where you in-other one another, freed

And ensphered where Love has cast out fear.

2. Circle Dance

A sun-warmed sapling, opening each leaf,
My soul unfolded in your quickening ray.
'The inner brought the outer into life',

I found the light within the light of day,
The Consolation of Philosophy,
Turning a page in Cambridge, found my way,

My mind delighting in discovery,
As love of learning turned to learning love
And explanation deepened mystery,

Drawing me out beyond what I could prove
Towards the next adventure. Every chance
Discovery a sweet come-hither wave,

Philosophy a kind of circle dance,
Weaving between the present and the past,
The whole truth present in a single glance

That looked on me and everything in Christ!
Threefold beholding, look me into being,
Make me in Love again from first to last,

And let me still partake your holy seeing
Beyond the shifting shadow of the earth;
Minute particulars, eternal in their being,

Forming themselves into a single path
From heaven to earth and back again to heaven,
All patterned and perfected, from each birth

To each fruition, and all freely given
To glory in and give the glory back!
Call me again to set out from this haven

And follow truth along her shining track.

3. The Rose

A white rose opens in a quiet arbour
Where I sit reading Dante. Paradise
Unfolding in me, opens hour by hour,

In sunlight and amidst the hum of bees
On a late afternoon. I think of how
Everything flowers: the whole universe

Itself is still unfolding even now,
Sprung from a stem of singularity
Which petals time and space. I think of how

The very elements that let my body be
Began and will continue in the stars
Whose light and distance frame our mystery,

And how my shadowed heart still loves, still bears
With every beat that animates my being,
Eternal yearnings through the turning years.

I turn back to the lines that light my seeing
And lift me to the limits of all thought
And long that I might also find that freeing

And enabling Love, and so be caught
And lifted into his renewing Heaven.
Evening glimmers and the stars come out.

Venus is shining clear. My prayers are woven
Into a sounding song, a symphony,
As all creation gives back what is given

In music made to praise the Mystery
Who is both gift and giver. Something stirs
A grace in me beyond my memory.

I close the book and look up at the stars.